15343

D1536191

teach me about

The Baby-Sitter

Childrens Press
School and Library Edition
Published 1987

Managing Editor: Ellen Klarberg
Copy Editor: Kate Dickey
Contributing Writer: Kathleen McBride
Contributing Editors: Libby Byers, Maureen Dryden, Yona Flemming
Editorial Assistant: Sandy Passarino

Art Director: Laurie Westdahl
Design and Production: Abigail Johnston
Illustrator: Bartholomew
Inker: Berenice Iriks
Production Assistant: Lillian Cram
Composition: Curt Chelin

teach me about

The Baby-Sitter

By JOY BERRY

Illustrated by Bartholomew

CHILDRENS PRESS ®

CHICAGO

Sometimes Mommy and Daddy

need to go out without me.

I need someone to take care

of me while they are gone.

Daddy and I are
going out for a while.

Mommy or Daddy asks a baby-sitter to take care of me. Sometimes the baby-sitter comes to my house.

My parents leave when

the baby-sitter comes.

Before Mommy and Daddy

leave, they tell

the baby-sitter and me

- where they will be going, and

- when they will be home.

The baby-sitter or I can call

Mommy or Daddy if we need to.

The baby-sitter does not want

me to get hurt.

The baby-sitter protects me

and tries to keep me safe.

The baby-sitter and I do things

that are fun together.

We play with my toys.

We play games.

We make things.

We read books.

13

Sometimes the baby-sitter

gives me food to eat.

15

Often the baby-sitter helps me

to take a bath and get dressed.

Sometimes the baby-sitter

puts me to bed.

17

The baby-sitter does not leave until Mommy and Daddy come home. There are times when Mommy and Daddy come home when I am still awake.

Other times Mommy and Daddy come home when I am asleep.

Sometimes Mommy or Daddy takes me to the baby-sitter's house.

There are many things

that are fun to do

at the baby-sitter's house.

- I play with toys.

- I play games.

- I make things.

- I read books.

Often I eat at the

baby-sitter's house.

23

Sometimes I nap

at the baby-sitter's house.

Sometimes the baby-sitter

does something that upsets me.

I tell the baby-sitter how I feel.

The baby-sitter talks with me,

and we work it out.

My mommy or daddy comes
to get me when it is time
for me to go home.

29

It is good to tell Mommy and

Daddy all about the baby-sitter

and the things we do together.

I tell them the things I like

about being with the baby-sitter.

I tell them the things

I do not like.

Mommy and Daddy want me

to feel happy and safe.

I tell them whether or not the

baby-sitter makes me feel

happy and safe.

This helps Mommy and Daddy

decide whether or not to ask

the baby-sitter to

take care of me again.

I am glad there is

a baby-sitter to take care of me

when Mommy and Daddy

are gone.